2, 95

This book may be kept

~~SEVEN DAYS~~

A fine will be charged for each
day the book is kept overtime.

FEB 9 1970 NO 03 '99		
JUL 14 72 AG 16 '70		
AUG 1 72		
AUG 21 72		
FEB 9 1974		
MAR 2 1976		
MAR 19 1976		
JUL 31 1976		
JY 15 '86		
JY 6 '87		
JA 17 '90 2/		
MR 25 9		
JY 01 '99		

More
To Collect
and Paint
from Nature

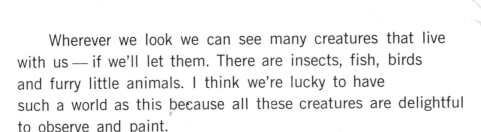

Wherever we look we can see many creatures that live with us — if we'll let them. There are insects, fish, birds and furry little animals. I think we're lucky to have such a world as this because all these creatures are delightful to observe and paint.

In this book I want to show you how to paint these living things — not how to paint them in a general way, but how to paint a particular one, using it as a model.

In some cases, you have the fun of collecting and keeping your model. In others, you will observe and perhaps take pictures with a camera.

In any case, I hope you will realize that in inviting you to an adventure in art and nature you will find no part of this adventure too easy. This does not mean it won't be fun nor does it mean that it is only for a few talented persons to paint well.

To be able to use a brush as a tool in painting is a physical thing. Anyone who can write can learn to use a brush. Observation is what really makes an artist. I can only show you how to handle a brush and suggest where you can look: the rest is up to your eyes.

More
To Collect
and Paint
from Nature

by JOHN HAWKINSON

ALBERT WHITMAN & COMPANY • CHICAGO

© 1964 by Albert Whitman & Company. L.C. Catalog Card Number 64-7715. Published simultaneously in Canada by George J. McLeod, Ltd., Toronto. Lithographed in the U.S.A.

MATERIALS

Good materials for painting are not expensive, but it is important to get the right kind.

Brushes

Although sable brushes are best to use, an inexpensive squirrel or ox-hair brush that sells for about fifty cents (Number 10 round) will do nicely. If you like, you can get other sizes too.

If you have brushes of different sizes, the size of the brush should determine the size of the painting.

Here is a painting of a robin made with a small brush and the same bird painted with a larger brush. The same strokes were used in each painting.

Brushes will last and keep their point for a longer time if you keep them clean and stand them in a jar when not in use.

This

The sure way to ruin the point of a brush is to leave it in your water jar.

Not This

Watercolors

Most of the commercial watercolor sets are much too small to use. Also, replacement pans are not too easily available.

If you take some small jar lids about one and one-half to two inches across (baby food jar lids are good) and glue them to a piece of wood, these lids can be filled and replenished when necessary with tube watercolors. I will not tell you which colors to use because I think this is something that you can find out best by yourself.

Full Pan

Round Pan

If you would rather buy a watercolor set, insist on the full pan size which is an oblong or large round pan. Avoid the little half pans.

Half Pan

Paper

In this book I have in most cases used paper that is available to you, even though I prefer rice paper. You can use newsprint, construction paper or any other fairly absorbent paper. Rice paper, although inexpensive, is hard to find. It is available at some large city art stores.

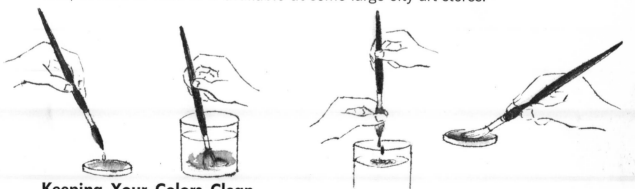

Keeping Your Colors Clean

When the color in a pan gets muddy from other color on the brush, add more water to the pan with the brush and work it to a soupy mixture. Then clean your brush in water and, with your fingers, gently squeeze out the water. With this dry brush pick up the muddy color from the pan.

BRUSH STROKES

When you paint with watercolor, the position of the body, how you sit, the position of the arm and how you hold the brush are all very important. The placement of the paper, water and color should make it easier for you to paint.

Sit erect in your chair, not too close to the table. Place the paper, water, brush, color and a piece of cloth or paper towel to clean your brush in front of you, as illustrated. If you are left-handed, everything should go on the left side of the paper.

Have your arm parallel to the table with the elbow held out, like this.

Dot Stroke

Hold the brush with the point vertical to the paper, as illustrated.

From this position, you can make dots by moving your arm up and down.

The press stroke is done from the same position. Just press the brush down, but look at the variation you can get with it. A wet brush, a dry brush, two or even three colors on the brush give you many changes.

Press Stroke

From the press stroke rotate the wrist slowly like this.

Press Wrist Stroke

If your brush strokes look like these, your movement is good.

If they look something like these, you are not holding the brush vertically or you are moving your fingers or arm.

Now try the same stroke with the brush this way.

If you move only your wrist, your strokes should look something like these.

If they look like these, try again and see that your brush is vertical.

Making Thin Lines

To make long thin lines, either curved or straight, the brush is held firmly and the finger and wrist do not move. Just the arm and elbow move. Try to feel the paper with the point of the brush. By keeping the arm parallel and the movement slow and graceful you can develop control in a very short time. If your brush skips and leaves blank spaces now and then, this just shows that you are doing it right.

Little Line Stroke

You may find it difficult to make short thin lines, but if you hold the brush low and let your little finger rest on the paper you will find it quite easy. Use a fairly dry brush.

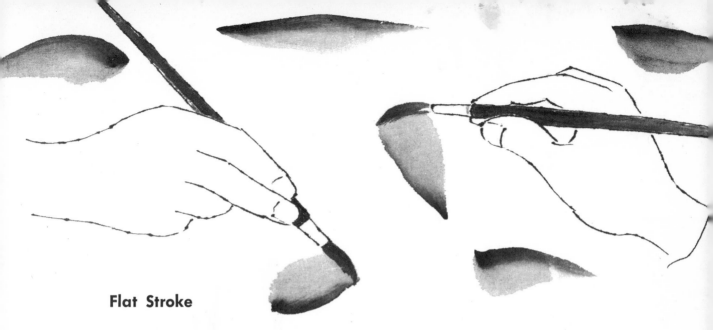

Flat Stroke

There are some strokes that are made with the brush held almost horizontal to the paper. The heel of the hand may rest on the paper. Whether you move just your fingers or wrist or arm, the tip of the brush should form a hard line on the paper while the heel of the brush may vary from thick to thin.

If you are right-handed it is natural to make strokes like this illustration.

It is extremely difficult to make strokes like this unless you turn the paper around. It can of course be done if you twist your hand about and then try to move the brush. But you will soon see why I recommend turning the paper. It is much easier than twisting your hand.

9

PAINTING A BUTTERFLY

The first adventure is the collecting, mounting and painting of a butterfly.

For the collecting you will need a net, a killing jar and a small box of shoe or cigar size.

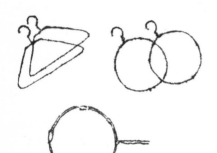

Here is how to make the net:

Take two wire coat hangers and bend them into a circle to make a ring.

Straighten the hooks and tape the two wire rings together.

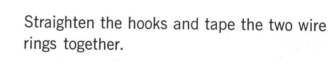

Use nylon or cotton netting and make a long, tapered bag about twenty inches long. The opening of the bag should be the same size as the wire rings.

Sew the bag on the wire rings.

Find a pole about three feet long and tie the net securely. Bamboo makes the best handle. It is light, and you can bend the short wires from the hooks to fit into the hollow bamboo.

Going on a butterfly safari is quite an adventure. I never realized what wonderful characters butterflies are until I tried to catch them. I found myself feeling glad for the ones that got away. After you catch three or four you can put away your net.

Live butterflies would be hard to use as models, so you must place your catch in a wide-mouthed jar that has a piece of cotton saturated with carbon tetrachloride (cleaning fluid). Over the cotton put a piece of heavy cardboard with a few holes punched in it.

After you catch a butterfly, put the net on the ground with a fold so that the insect cannot escape.

Open the lid of the jar and put it on the ground next to the net.

Reach in and take hold of the butterfly.

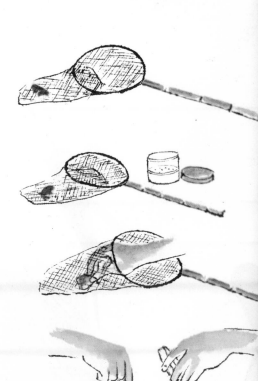

Put it into the jar and close the lid. After the butterfly stops moving, remove it and put it in the box.

Butterflies should be mounted soon after you catch them or they will become too brittle to handle. Don't wait more than one or two days.

To mount a butterfly as a model for painting, gently fix the wings in a flying position or a resting position. With a little household cement, attach a pipe cleaner to the underside of the body. Put a bit of modeling clay at the other end of the pipe cleaner and your model is ready to paint.

Place the butterfly in front of you on a table. Adjust it until you get a view that you like.

Arrange your paper, color, brush and water as described on page 6. Add a drop or two of water to each pan of color to soften it. Try blending the colors on the brush. For instance, if your model is orange, saturate the side of the brush in yellow, then dip the point in red. Apply this to the paper and see what happens. The trick is to use just the right amount of water, and only trying will tell you how much is right.

The front wings of a butterfly can be painted with a press stroke (page 7) or by moving the finger with the heel of the hand resting on the paper (page 9). Try both ways.

The back wings are easy. Just use press strokes, as described at the top of page 7.

After the wings, paint the butterfly body with one short stroke. Wait until the wings are almost dry before adding details. This can be done easiest by using the little finger as a helper, as shown at the bottom of page 8.

Now there isn't much sense in having a model if you don't use it. So while your hand is concentrating on the brush, let your eyes concentrate on the butterfly. This is not nearly as difficult as it sounds after you have developed a rhythm to your stroke. The tendency at the beginning is to be too fast and jerky. Be slow and easy in your movements and the skill you want will surely come.

It's only the first butterflies that are hard to paint. Then it becomes fun. And you can use the models you have for painting other butterflies you see. All you have to remember is their color and markings. Here are some different kinds of butterflies and moths. See if you can recognize the brush strokes.

INSECTS

In the country, in your backyard or at a nearby empty lot you can find crickets, grasshoppers, beetles and other insects to catch in your hand. Some insects, like grasshoppers and crickets, can be kept for a short time in a cricket cage. They can be fed grass or leaves. Many insects that live on smaller insects must be used as models immediately.

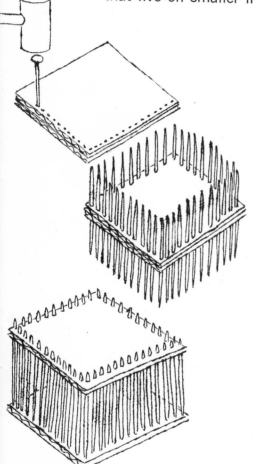

A cricket cage is easy to make. Cut two pieces of corrugated cardboard about three inches square. With a small nail punch holes one-fourth inch apart around the outside edge. The two pieces of cardboard should be held together when punched so that the holes will match.

Next insert toothpicks, as in the illustration. Then pull the cardboards apart to form the cage and put a touch of glue on each toothpick to hold it in place. Two toothpicks should be left unglued for a gate.

If you have difficulty seeing the insect to paint in the cage, you can transfer it to a box with a glass lid.

Here are some insects painted with simple brush strokes. How the brush strokes are done is described at the bottom of the page and numbered. Corresponding numbers are positioned around the insects to show you where the brush strokes are used.

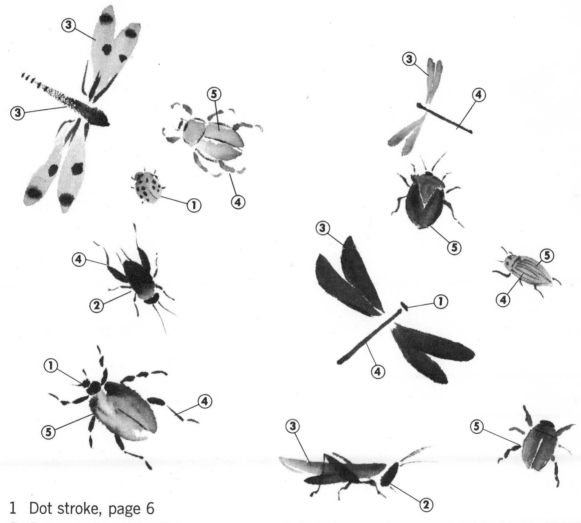

1 Dot stroke, page 6
2 Press stroke, page 7
3 Press wrist stroke, page 7
4 Little line stroke, bottom of page 8
5 Flat stroke, page 9

FISH

In lakes and streams you can find what are generally called panfish — bluegills, sunfish, goggle-eye, perch, striped bass and rock bass.

Panfish are fun to catch, lots of fun to keep and wonderful to paint. To carry fish home from where you catch them, use a large pail of water and add ice cubes, one at a time. Fish tabs, sold for about fifteen cents at bait shops, are also good to supply oxygen.

The fish can be kept in an aquarium. Some of them will take bits of hamburger from the tip of your finger. Of course, if you have a fish that is fairly big he may take a bit of your finger, too.

To keep panfish in an aquarium you will have to separate the fish with rocks or screening to stop them from fighting. Except for this, they take the same care that other fish do. Don't overfeed. If you live where water is chlorinated, let it stand overnight before using. Don't overcrowd the aquarium — one or two fish are enough.

A fish seems made to order for brush strokes. Depending on the size, the body can be painted in one or two strokes.

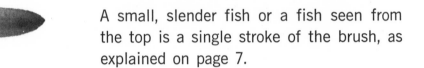

A small, slender fish or a fish seen from the top is a single stroke of the brush, as explained on page 7.

Details like eyes and fins can be added with dot and press strokes.

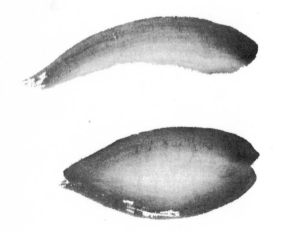

Most panfish will require two strokes for the body. The back can be painted with two colors on the brush. Then the underside is painted with the same stroke. You may find it easier to turn the paper when doing this. Use the stroke described at the top of page 9.

The tail stroke is similar to a butterfly wing. The fin can be painted with a simple press stroke.

Let the painting become almost dry before adding details such as stripes, gills and eyes — again using a rather dry brush.

BIRDS

Birds are beautiful and graceful and should be fun to paint. Unfortunately they won't sit still for us.

Here are some birds that you can see in your yard, in a park or on a trip in the country. Because they will not sit still to model for you they will be difficult to paint. So on the following pages are instructions for painting a parakeet. The brush strokes for a parakeet and his wild cousins are basically the same. The bill, the color and size may be different for wild birds, but they all sit on a twig in much the same way.

Begin with a Parakeet

If you have a parakeet that will sit on your finger and pose while you are painting him you will be lucky. It's more likely that the bird will start to play with your brush and you will have to be content with painting him in his cage.

If you don't have a parakeet, perhaps you have a friend who has one and will let you use it for a model.

Here is a photograph of a parakeet and the brush strokes for the head, the breast, the wings and tail.

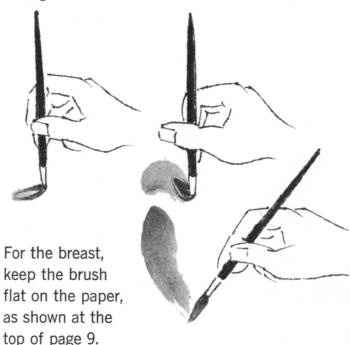

For the head, use a press stroke, then twist the brush in your fingers.

For the breast, keep the brush flat on the paper, as shown at the top of page 9.

The wing is a press wrist stroke shown on page 7.

The tail feathers are press wrist strokes. Don't press all the way down. Start at the end of the tail and paint toward the body.

The eyes, feet and other details are dot and short line strokes. Wait until the paint is almost dry.

With the exception of the details, these strokes do not have to follow any particular order. It is better to practice each stroke to your satisfaction before trying to paint the whole bird.

To Paint a Pigeon

I don't suppose there are many of us who don't live close to some pigeons—many people I know think they live a little too close. But I like pigeons and I hope that you do, too, for they are such beautiful birds to paint.

Pigeons are friendly. Take some peanuts to the park and you may have some birds feed from your hand. This should give you the chance to observe a pigeon's colors, character and shape.

If you take some photographs of these pigeons they will be of tremendous help when you paint them. The brush strokes are similar to the ones you used for the parakeet.

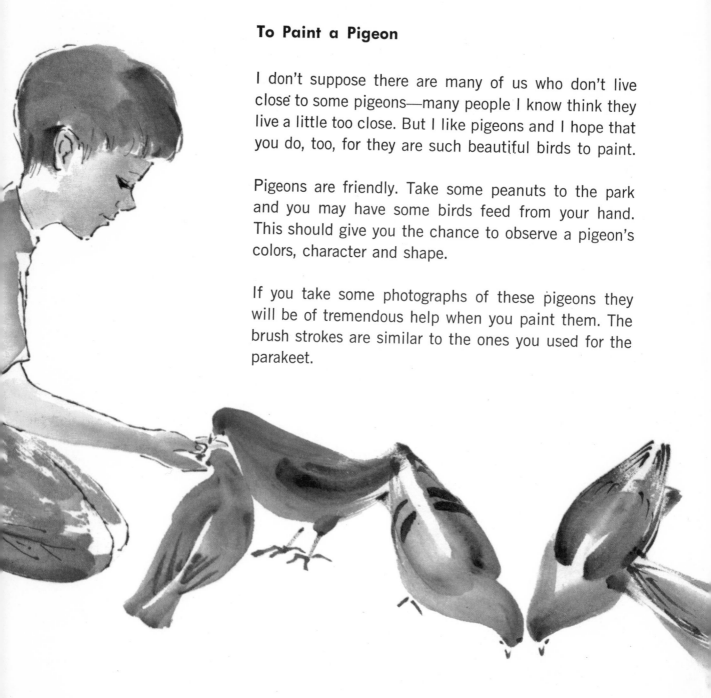

To get the beautiful blend of colors on the head and neck will take practice, but try it. Dip your brush in the colors that you remember and see what happens.

The breast is the same stroke that you used for a parakeet. The wings are painted with the same stroke as the butterfly wing.

Start the tail strokes at the end and paint toward the body. Use a press wrist stroke and a fairly dry brush.

The beak and the feet can be done by making short lines, using your little finger to help keep the lines thin and sharp.

Other details, such as dark wing bars, should be added when the other strokes are dry.

There are other birds, like chickens and ducks, that we can observe closely on a farm or at a zoo. The brush strokes for a chicken or duck are much the same as for a pigeon.

The comb on the head of the rooster is done with a press stroke using a fairly dry brush to get the points. The neck can be painted with three or four press wrist strokes. For the body and wing, use the stroke described on page 9.

Tail feathers of a rooster are long and swirly. Start with a press wrist stroke and then give your brush a twist. It's lots of fun.

The duck's head is started with a press stroke. Then the brush is twisted for the neck. Try press strokes for the ducklings.

Don't forget that you can take snapshots of ducks and chickens at farms and zoos.

Flying Birds

No matter where you live you will find birds that spend most of their lives flying in the air above you. In the city or the country, there are many birds that you can see and enjoy by just watching them fly. You can also look at these birds for the purpose of remembering and painting.

Painting flying birds is not a thing that you can do in a short time. It will take hours of observation and some work with the brush to paint a bird with a feeling of flight.

In the spring and all summer we can enjoy watching the swallows, the swifts and the purple martins fly in the sky above us. Here are many opportunities to observe them for painting.

Chimney swifts are little birds with long, sharp wings and hardly any tail at all. They flit around in happy little flocks.

The body of a chimney swift can be done with one stroke of the wrist and their wings in one stroke, again using the wrist. See page 7.

The martins and swallows are the most graceful of these flying birds. If you have a martin house in your neighborhood, you can get a close view of their beautiful flying maneuvers. The wings are similar in shape to the front wings of a butterfly and can be painted in the same way.

Here are two other birds that we can all see flying overhead, the nighthawks and the gulls.

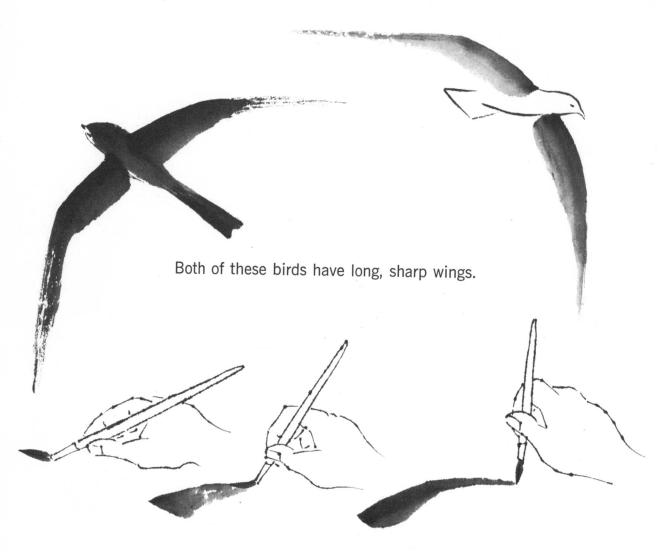

Both of these birds have long, sharp wings.

Paint the inner part of the wing by keeping the brush flat on the paper. Then without taking the brush off the paper, lift the hand to an almost vertical position and paint the outer part of the wing by moving your wrist away from you.

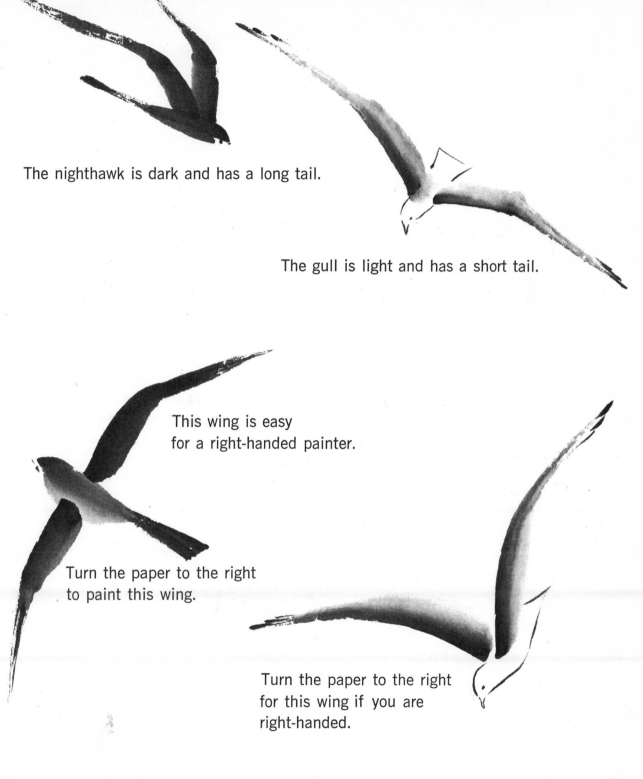

The nighthawk is dark and has a long tail.

The gull is light and has a short tail.

This wing is easy
for a right-handed painter.

Turn the paper to the right
to paint this wing.

Turn the paper to the right
for this wing if you are
right-handed.

SQUIRRELS

Squirrels are about the only wild animals that we all see close up no matter where we live.

If you live in the city, you might take a bag of peanuts, perhaps a camera, and go to the nearest park. There you will be sure to find squirrels to feed, watch and take pictures of. It is nice to have someone along to help you.

If you get good photographs, they can be useful when you are painting. If you don't have a camera or your pictures are not very good, you can use the pictures in this book. But before you do, go and look at squirrels. There is no substitute for seeing for yourself.

From a photograph let me show you the brush strokes I use in painting a squirrel.

For the head, try a press stroke.

For the ears, press just the tip of a fairly dry brush.

For the body, mold with the brush flat on the paper. The front paws can be press wrist strokes.

The tail is a press wrist stroke done with a swirl of the fingers. Use a wet brush with lots of color on the point.

Use dots for the eye and nose and little lines for the claws.

Of course the pictures you take and the observations you make may be different from the example on page 35. Here are some photographs and paintings that may come closer to yours.

As you can see, painting this way does not give you an exact copy of the photograph. But with the observations you make and the grace of your brush strokes, you can get action and character into your painting.

There are other places to find animals to see and paint. You may have a pet mouse or rabbit at home. If not, at the children's zoos you can see and hold small animals like these. It may be difficult for you to paint the animal at the zoo, but close observation and remembering will help when you get home.

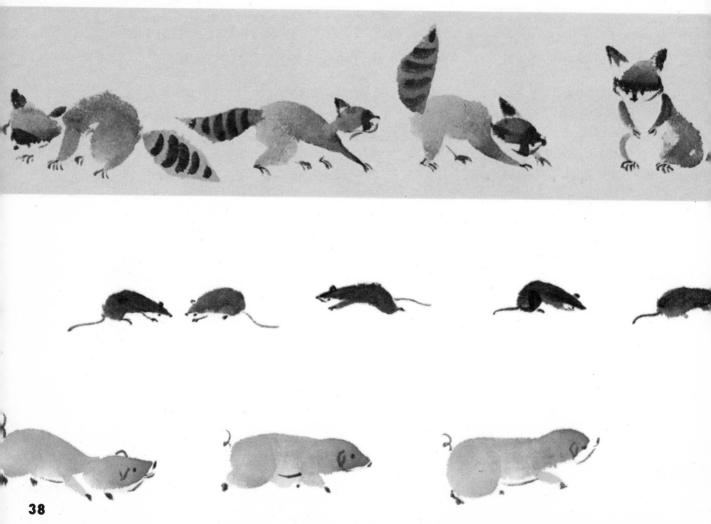

When you are able to take trips to the woods look for different animal life. Depending on where and when you go, there are chipmunks, red squirrels and rabbits. All these animals can be painted with the same brush strokes used for the gray squirrel.

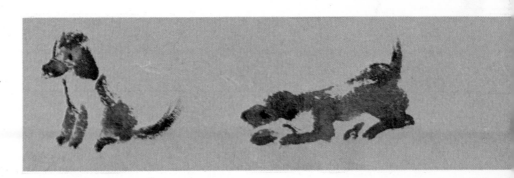

To help you identify the insects, birds, and animals shown in this book . . .

Pages 14-15: Cabbage butterfly, red admiral, wood nymph, clouded sulphur, viceroy, mourning cloak, monarch, silver blue, red-spotted purple, bronze copper, portia, leto fritillary, northern metalmark, black swallowtail

Page 17: Dragonfly, damselfly, cricket, grasshopper, stinkbug, ladybug, beetles

Pages 18-19: Perch, sunfish, striped bass, bluegill, crappie

Pages 22-23: Robin, goldfinch, cardinal, blue jay, song sparrow

Pages 30-31: Chimney swift, barn swallow, cliff swallow, bank swallow, purple martin

Pages 32-33: Nighthawk, herring gull

Pages 38-39: Chipmunk, dog, raccoon, mouse, pig, sheep, rabbit, bear, dog, deer

*The author wishes to thank Leroy Lahman
for his help with the photographic illustrations.*